IN THE
KOSHER CHOW MEIN RESTAURANT

Claire,

Very best wishes !

Roger May

Also by Roger Nash

Settlement in A School of Whales (poetry)
Psalms from the Suburbs (poetry)
Night Flying (poetry)
Ethics, Science, Technology and the Environment:
    Reader (philosophy)
Ethics, Science, Technology and the Environment:
    Study Guide (philosophy)
The Poetry of Prayer (literary criticism and
    philosophy)

IN THE
KOSHER CHOW MEIN RESTAURANT

Roger Nash

Your Scrivener Press

Canadian Cataloguing in Publication Data

Nash, Roger, 1942-
    In the Kosher Chow Mein Restaurant

Poems
ISBN 1-896350-02-X

    I. Title

PS8577.A73I6 1996   C811'.54   C96-900188-6
PR9199.3.N38I6 1996

Book design: Laurence Steven
Cover photos: Caedmon and Chris Nash

Published by *Your Scrivener Press*
465 Loach's Road, Sudbury, Ontario, Canada,
P3E 2R2

For my sons,

Piers and Caedmon

ACKNOWLEDGEMENTS

"In the Kosher Chow Mein Restaurant" won First Prize in *Fiddlehead*'s 1993-1994 Poetry Contest.

Some of these poems have appeared previously in:

Antigonish Review ("Ageing gracefully", "1942", "Maxims for marriages")

Arc ("Circumstantial evidence of the visitation of angels")

Ariel ("Letter read in a storm", "Heavy rain", "Bell-ringing", "Vagaries of memory at mid-winter")

Canadian Author and Bookman ("The house-burning")

Canadian Literature ("Vinnie", "Heritage")

Dandelion ("Betting on history", "Street of gold", "An old man remembers a hard winter in his youth", "The girl in musical jeans")

Event ("The appliances delivery-man")

Fiddlehead ("A message from the Norns to the twenty-first century", "In the Kosher Chow Mein Restaurant")

Malahat Review ("Old man in an armchair", "Parting", "Means and ends", "Preparations for a journey", "Presences as absences")

Outlook, Jewish Outlook Society ("Borders")

Poetry Canada Review ("A desperate woman", "Marriage of opposites", "My lady of journeys", "Where our voices go")

Quarry ("Letter home while working in the bush")

Queen's Quarterly ("Chicken-plucking")

The Garden of Life, National Library of Poetry, U.S.A., ("Trying to balance the books")

Wascana Review ("The strong wind")

Windsor Review ("Geraniums", "Wind-bells can overcome jealousy", "Six reversals", "Superstitions", "Phrases of the moon", "My mother")

Contents

Chicken-Plucking

Circumstantial Evidence of the Visitation of Angels

The Street of Gold

A Message From the Norns to the Twenty-First Century

In the Kosher Chow Mein Restaurant

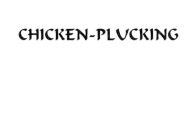

CHICKEN-PLUCKING

Geraniums

Geraniums once kept a houseful
of my maiden aunts. They hogged
all the bright spots
by the windows, growing hairier
and fat, elbowing out the sun.
My aunts were edged inexorably
back into the stone-cold
interiors of their rooms. There,
they moved gently in the perpetual
dark, making a barely
discernible glow with their watering
cans, spending virtually
days each hour in attentive
incantations. Those geraniums vaulted
vigorously upward into the years,
sweating unashamedly over the steamed-up
windows, giving off an odour
as thick as burning toast,
though laced with the juice of lemons.
My aunts, proud to be just so
accommodating, grew as transparent
and thin as potato tubers,
meandering in as many opposite
directions through their sunless rooms,
selflessly adjusting and readjusting,
until the day the geraniums chucked
the very last of them out.

A desperate woman

The stars were hopelessly inconsistent with her as a
        child,
giving nothing but double messages.
They granted her, in a simultaneously soft yet haughty
light, only the half-magic
of making things immensely desirable
because they are a long way off.
That glittering grid of causes winked
confusedly, and the assuagement of her sharpest pangs
became overwhelmingly elsewhere, as if on another
unnamed, unnumbered and still undiscovered planet.
Tonight, in the rain on the patio, an unplanted
rose is trying to open. That balustrade,
was it always broken? She smiles at her so closely
absent husband, over the supper table.
A pistol points tenderly but decisively
out of her eyes. At last, the catch
is off. It's a hold-up. She is desperate
to force both him and the rain to come
with her willingly. The rising stars wink on,
their light as aloof yet as softening as ever before.

Letter read in a storm

Windows twitched, then stuttered in their frames,
muttering up an approaching storm.

Outside, two butterflies boiled
their wings over against a yellowing pane.

Clouds were coiffured crazily atop
each other. Lightening toppled tiaras down.

Inside, her eyes drew themselves up
to their full length. She opened the letter

with the whole of her face. Suddenly, the room
went black as boot polish,

and gravel in the driveway threw up
fistful after fistful of knuckle-white rain.

Her face snapped. Beads from her broken
necklace pattered all over the floor.

Flowers in a bowl, sweetpeas
from his garden, clutched absentmindedly at her hand,

and broke its fingers between them, gently,
one by one, dropping them onto the carpet.

A year after he was missing in action,
that official letter came. Unofficially,

two last yellow butterflies
were left to limp away across the lawn.

The house-burning

This morning, the old Finnish house
across the lake burned itself to the ground.
With unashamed speed, having longed for this moment
through generations of hard, prim winters,
heads splintering with sleep at prayer
by the kitchen table, it suddenly drew on
every red dress ever
dreamed of by its long-departed women,
returning them to an unexpressed eagerness, a gasp
along their thighs. The chimneys slipped into
          embroidered
sleeves that rippled against the sky. Windows
flew out yellow silk scarves.
The whole building swayed past
the sweating birches in a diaphanous cape
of sparks. So self-completing this beauty,
none of us, barely awakened and merely
men, circling with fire-axes
and sharply-edged eyes hefting
wildly, could come close or yet leave her. Lifetimes
of lost longings from the long-consumed
women-folk billowed out in a last
voluptuous sunflower gown of flame,
stalked on a wind twirling breathlessly
upward from the bright, curling pages
of their now unclasped diaries.

Superstitions

One evening, after her husband, yet again,
had tried to be gentle by only beating her
extremely lightly, she promptly turned
into another of his superstitions, and flew out
of the window as a small brown owl,
suddenly eager and light of wing,
her sure instinct lighting up
the broken bones of their life like an inescapable
X-ray. In the empty apartment,
he was horrified to find the mirrors gave
no clear reflections. The next morning,
he awoke as a cold sober, but elaborately
unlucky, number. Even black cats
hurled themselves under cars, rather than cross
his path. Now, a year later,
she is just beginning to outgrow his superstitions.
At Mardi Gras, she discreetly tucks her feathers
under the mask of a very regal lady,
and leaves by the side door, to join
the crowds under stars that rise like the unstoppable
notes of a pennilessly happy saxophone.

My lady of journeys

A man waits by a door to meet a woman
as poised as the plates from China inside her room,
as quiet and collected as the wall they rest upon.
And she shows him her laughter, that she lives in so
    wisely.
And she shows him her hair, charged with storms in
    the mountains.
But she does not show him how her eyes can see
    beyond
his future into the past, where she has learned the
    reasons
for weeping, and for never withholding her singing and
    dancing.
And he decides never to decide on anything until after
it happens, as the paths in her dishes wander beyond
the clouds above the Yangtze river. Then a peasant
waves from a bridge that they should come over and be
    him,
while the fish in the river begin to jump in her
    laughter,
and the potatoes start to boil on her stove for their
    supper,
until he breaks out of the last of his burst skins.
Then they eat at a table set on one of the bridges,
where they tell stories to each other that he finds in the
    night,
with no surprise, are the streets in his dreams. And he
    waits
for her in one, by a door that is as damp with rain as a
    pillow.
It opens as fragrantly as the cherry blossoms in her
    voice,

and he enters its endless distances, deciding on nothing
until after it happens, as she puts his longing poems
in a quietening drawer, and lies down to sleep
beside all of the reasons for her singing and dancing.

My mother

At weekends, she dusted photos on her mantelpiece,
then readjusted them carefully. Edge to edge:
sons working on different parts
of the globe, brothers in retirement on different
sides of the grave. She was tracing the length
of the tip of the nail on God's little
finger, as it dipped and moved in our lives.

As a widow, she baked raisin-bread
just once a week. Her two hands
kneaded patiently in the mixing bowl.
And her other two hands she held
in silent prayer at her chin. So that yeast
throughout the universe would work well, with an
            absolutely
even distribution of raisins in life.

My mother knew that, at the end of a day,
tired language must be put away
like an apple-pie, and laid out
for watering mouths the next morning.
Then miracles can be described, and so continue to
            occur.
Including the not inconsiderable miracle
of words in thick cream for breakfast.

The girl in musical jeans

As she walks down the street,
photographs fall out
of albums in front rooms.
Ormolu clocks start
by themselves, for the first time
this century. As she sways past
the bill-boards, they peel.
She is the only authorized advertisement
for sunset. Then, as she turns
the corner, the way she moves
instantly retunes every
single piano in town.

Ageing gracefully

At ninety-three, she cat-naps cautiously
into the brittle afternoons. Even
the brass bedstead can overtake her.
It rolls vigorously forward
into the mirror. But everything waits for her there.
She's learned what to use mirrors for.
When her skin looks more
wrinkled and streaked with dust
than is usual, her reflection just
smiles reprovingly, and brushes
her down with its feather duster.

Chicken-plucking

In their village above the sea, the old women
sit together on stools in the shade,
plucking chickens for this evening's festival.
When the wind blows, their words fly
everywhere—even across the waves—and get into
everything. They gather them together, washing
and then drying them, so that their mouths can go on
          whispering
inside the new brides' pillows, night
after night, plumping these up with advice
and consolation. Their gossip only tickles the noses
of children. Will it? Will it make them sneeze?

When they push their cool, dry hands
into the slaughtered hens, pulling out
warm guts, it is as though God Herself
reached carefully into Her curious creation,
through the pitch-forked hole in the stomach
of Her nearby, feverish, farm-labourer.
But She sees only what the old women
see: fire burning thistles
and dead grass on the hill-side;
injustice and a lack of mercy under the trees.

Afterwards, reading the entrails, they see
with the reddening eyes of sunset shining
through keyholes. The drying entrails form,
in the dust, a most detailed archaeology
of their daughters' futures. Yet they are, equally,
          prophecies
of marriages the women themselves would prefer
to have made in the past. The old men

go on sneezing, quietly and forgivingly.
After all, they must spit in the same dust.
They, too, accept the ancient rules
of chicken-plucking, that no-one has completely
explained to them: the rules of weight and pleasure;
of witnesses and the suddenly dead; and of how the
       heart
can nevertheless scrape a living, with feathers
and a weekly bowl of chicken soup.

CIRCUMSTANTIAL EVIDENCE
OF THE VISITATION OF ANGELS

Maxims for marriages

Whoever has a tall wife
won't need ladders.
If you have a dark-haired wife,
you'll never lack jam.
If you have a wife who laughs,
there'll always be rivers.
Should she have untucked eyes,
the house will be warm.

Whoever has a thin husband
won't need curtains.
If he has rough hands,
the stars will clear the roof.
Suppose he has a grey hair,
there'll always be oceans.
Should he be a man who listens,
even trees will kiss you on the mouth.

Whoever has a tall ladder
will never lack jam.
If you have a dark-haired laugh,
you'll always be a river.
As the stars have grey hair,
we'll listen to each other.
And until the curtains clear the roof,
we'll untuck the oceans in one another.

What my love is not

My love is like a chili pepper,
she spices my days so good.
My love is like a stove in fall,
chock-a-block with wood.
My love is like the clover bloom,
I can taste her all over our valley.
My love is like the coyote's call,
she's hungry for the moon.
But one thing my love is not,
is a goddam sickly sweet
merely garden rose.

Marriages of opposites

In the laboratories of the spirit, marriages of opposites
conduct their crucial experiments, showing how
this contradictory world is just about possible.
Because of the sundering unions, the consummated
partings, in the longest lasting of their beds,
the dead tree in the garden and the green
tree in the garden are the same tree,
and April is the month. Gold in the river
shines indistinguishably from mud.   The rich
are burdened by the poverty of their wealth. People
and mountains can speak the same language.
The compassionate are often the most cruel;
and peace declares war on itself.
In marriages of opposites, the saving evidence
is that those who are culpably ignorant of each other
are the ones who know each other best.

The military history of love

As you soaped in the bubble-bath, foam
flecked once more the flanks of a mare
running eagerly to meet trumpets
and war-horses of an ancient king.

Some nights, we lay awake on my back, listening
to sleepless chains failing to hold back
a sleeping mastiff from its dreams, as it stormed
towering white throats of rabbits.

When we walked out each morning, tailors' dummies
in store windows hurled shadows
into the advancing snow like hand-grenades.

We made love while tea in the samovar brewed,
but had usually forgotten to put in the tea.
We'd have argued whose fault, even if a ram's horn
had blown for the end of the world—leaving
one cup of water to meet our Maker.

Parting

Already, rain is being drawn up
in waterspouts far out at sea
that won't reach us both together,
with its usual clatter of soft nails,
you trying to dry your hair
while lying beside my open thoughts.

The sofa in the hotel constantly rearranges
its cushions, as though no one had ever sat there.
New sheets give the bed
amnesia. There are dates now forming
at the back of the calendar when you will not have
to try to remember to try to forget me.

The journeys we will take move in opposite
directions to our hands and eyes. Towns on
your way fill their names with streets
of unpronounceable dust. Already, when you walk
across the room, the air closes with a snap
in the eddies behind your fast-moving skirt.

Last night, the moon calmly calculated
a high tide that will not rise
for us together. Our footprints on the beach will be
            carefully
subtracted, and we will walk slowly backwards
among streets of amorous and inquisitive fishes
with luminous languages instead of eyes,

to separate rooms in a place before we met.
I wait there, with memories too happy to have
            happened yet.

Letter home while working in the bush

I want you when you pour thick tea
into the tallest glasses, me sipping through a sugarlump
held in my teeth, while your scented voice
stirs gently round and round
in any tall stem I might call my mind.

I want you in the last dance, my lips
drinking dew from the early morning
of your ears, and the whole dance floor
trembling, your green dress waltzing
three feet to one side of our eyes.

And I want your eyes, absorbing darkness
in their cries, then turning it to voodoo orchids
of light. And I want you under that dreadfully untidy
kitchen table, golden stars
rising in the grain and firmament of maple.

I want you even in my grandma's attic,
the cistern beside us singing all the truths
and untruths ever known to water. And I want you
when I was five, and had never yet met you, so my
        past
can catch up on the way your knees smile.

I want you in the Zinn desert, where the mating
camel, when he sees someone watching, follows
him home and chews the splintering door
right through in the sheer injustice
of his interrupted, was that it? Passion. I want you

in Tel Aviv, in Cairo, in Rome,

but first of all, in Wanup, Ontario.

My guitar is tuned to bears gently
stealing garbage; my voice to the sound
of crows giving warning of a clairvoyant truck
parked in the forest, the excited insides
of its windows both icing and steaming up.

Wind-bells can overcome jealousy

As you bent to kiss me,
your ear-lobes and wrists
tinkled and shone
with gifts from admirers
before we'd met.
Though the wind went on blowing,
our wind-bells suddenly
stopped. But then, reassuringly,
the bells went on chiming,
though the wind had stopped.

Family resemblances

My sons have my wife's eyes,
her brothers' courage and aversion
to prayers, my great-grandfather's
composure in any leather
chair, after supper,
shining his shoulders against the
aching metal studs.
When they look thoughtful,
they stand like trees in the garden.
It is unclear to our friends how
genetics has made use of me.
Yet I once looked like the coatstand
in the corner deli, gangling
and dusty; which has the abandoned air
of a bent umbrella; which rebuffs
expectation like souffles that catch
fire in the kitchen; which are as surprising
as my wife's soft breasts;
which operate my feet toward her thighs
when a scroll unrolls its script
of ancient love from her eyes.
And my sons have my wife's eyes.

Disagreements with Descartes

To love   is to enter reality
Skies range   from rain to sun to sleet again
I love   therefore I am
(Amo   ergo sum)
We love   therefore we
am (Amamus   ergo sum)
            one
Snow   pulls down thick blinds
on our window   but tips in a churn of
      light

Epithalamion for a silent Quaker wedding

During the wordless Quaker wedding,
the absence of an organ played a delicate
fretwork of fugues on the streaming sunlight;
while the shy and the rather hard of hearing
sat side by side, and communed at length,
without their lips ever moving.
At that silent ceremony, there was a ceaseless crowd
of unfalling footsteps. For the yet unborn
and already dead were also invited.

In the exchange of vows, only meadow-larks
and deer could speak for the bride. Though a rooster
coughed so discreetly, and affirmatively,
from behind a stand of trees. Quarter-horses
answered for the groom, neighing in harmony
—six-part, I think—from the edge
of the greenest field. Blackflies, as is traditional,
gave their unswerving consent to everything that
           moved;
and then, afterwards, to everything that stayed still.

When banjo and accordion began to play
at the reception, numerous cherubim were spotted
around the coffee-urn, flapping their wings
in time. Though no coffee was turned
into wine, there was a seven-fold increase
in the steps we are urged to dance our lives along.

As the bride cut the cake with care,
she arranged exactly equal slices
like a row of well-shelved books

in some lost library of Atlantis.
They contained the enduring knowledge that love,
like cake, can leave not a crumb behind.

That evening, coyotes across the valley struck up
the world's oldest kazoo orchestra,
ensuring that all of the blessings were blessed.
Hills inclined the caverns of their ears.
They listen for us after everyone is asleep.

Circumstantial evidence of the visitation of angels

On the evidence of one hill
and several passing clouds,
there were only two of them.
Under an unprepared, but nevertheless
dark blue sky,
they met by the trees at the edge
of the field. Her cotton dress
rustled, and seemed eager
to cast shadows entirely
on its own. His forehead was uncertain.
Her eyes and freckled knees
were absolutely final. They walked
through the tall grasses of the field,
and lay down in them. After that,
we couldn't see properly.
But there was a tumult of red hair,
and nearly grey. It was as though
the whole field revolved
around them, like a water-wheel
urged on by eager oxen.
They came to have at least
six legs, and wings
from nowhere. They performed feats
like charioteers, or cherubim on bicycles.
When they left, the whole field
was doing deep breathing
and floating exercises. Afterwards,
there were no sad animals.
But the sky was completely abandoned,
along with one high-heeled
shoe in the grass, which still

fills, after rain, with cherubim
peddling clouds like bicycles.

THE STREET OF GOLD

Vinnie

Vinnie DiSanto aged eight from the Bronx
visiting a farm for an uncle's funeral
heard clouds bleat distinctly
fields strut then crow yellow
corn at the dawn saw goats
mow grass while backfiring badly
from their twostroke tails and skunks mace
every old lady repeatedly
for stealing the huckleberries discovered geese
clashed gears when anyone tried
to think tractors gambolled and noon
fought fields then buried their dead
coyotes' cries pickpocketed
his dreams each night until he was glad
to get safely home again and camp
in the comfort of his favourite burnedout car
a yellow rain drumming on its crusted
roof the way rain should

The appliances delivery-man

At the thunderclap snap of his fingerbolt hands,
stoves shifted sideways to their proper
shapes, with never a sign of a scratch.
Yet his wife's smile dented
on her gold-filled teeth, nervous under
the lumbering kindness of his touch. While his
        thumbs
grew as thick as fly-blown
sausages, she went as thin as a dull
tin plate. When she left him, and he took
to whisky, no-one thought to count
the hundreds of leg-weaving cats
which, with great trembling efforts of steps
and nozzles of sweat, he had successfully never
built into carpets to basements. What rubbery
pups escaped being sieved through flagstones
into a kibbling dark, unmade before an incoming
new furnace, his shirt stuck
as far as the inside of his lungs in the soaking
grey-flannel air? And who knows
what angry words he masterfully manhandled
into not being spoken, stacked in a back
room of his life, along with the faulty heating
ducts? Only, perhaps, the huge
eye of the sky on summer afternoons,
heat as wavy as washboards, staring
unblinking down on straining staves
and pickets in his barrel-back, refusing
to give shade, or anything else, away.

To a company president, on his forty-ninth birthday at fifty

On his forty-ninth birthday at fifty,
he announced to his assembled staff that they were,
as usual, mistaken: he had decided to remain
a dynamic year short of half
a century—though he'd accept their mounded tributes
anyway. As he spoke, milled gravel
in the company driveway clicked quietly together,
reassembling itself slowly as rocks and boulders.
Then, by executive memo, all the fragments
of ships throughout history, that sank on their way
to promised lands, began to arrive
at their ports of origin, even the holes in their sails.
As he left through the foyer, he effortlessly ascended
the indoor waterfall, with rapidly increasing
muscles in his arms, returning to the source,
speeding indifferently past the spawning
fishes—who are inexplicably addicted to exhaustion
and dying—letting himself into the elegant
icefields with a master key, and then closing
a cubicled glacier behind him with a robust slam.
Inside, and carefully reversing the hands
on his underinsured watch, he suddenly discovers
micky-mouse go an wanna see mamma.

Memories of a settler

They walked across a new land. It was so
large, each footstep promptly forgot itself.
In that first winter, the date palms
of his childhood home got thoroughly blanketed
by the more freshly fallen memories of snow.
Yes, new memories drifted
high for several years around him, until what
he had hoped to become was the best he could make
        out
clearly from his past. One summer,
even the green minarets of his youth
became bears' eyes in the endless forest;
and the sun-smacked shutters of a small
white house softened into the plumage
of owls. The house began to blink,
and flew away. In the end, he took a warming
look from the snows, as though they were crumpled
sheets from a recent love-making. His wife
in the new land took from his eyes
in their creaking bed the remarkable gift
of moving as saltily as the sea, as frenziedly
as a fig tree in a thunder storm,
lightening flashing on all her breasts
and leaves. At last, what he had been
became what he now was. And when he lay dying,
he had fully achieved not knowing
exactly where he was. When the telegram arrived
at his place of birth, announcing his death,
the bears snapped promptly back
into mosques again, as though they had never been
        anything
else. But the green minarets kept a tense

ambiguity, always ready to re-open
their almond-shaped eyes; the muezzins' calls
ambling gently through the shaggy desert
air, singing from the forests of Paradise.

An old man remembers a hard winter in his youth

The coldest winters are always in the past.
In Poland, even star-light can freeze
before it hits the ground. I went
to the barn, to fetch in wood. Katerina,
the maid, was chopping away at a block,
killing a hen; her strong breasts
both breaking the laws of gravity.
Quite apart from the cold, I was shivering
with need for her. My uncle came out and caught us
at it. He beat me so hard,
the snow stopped for that winter. And gravity
has definitely been pulling harder at my ankles
every cold winter since.

Bell-ringing at evening

In the sleeping cathedral town, an avalanche
of bells swept heavily down.
Iron boulders formed instantly
out of mid-air, and fell mercilessly upon the backs
of burghers. Only birds got swung
to safety overhead, on taut ropes
fraying in the palms of steeples. At the marketplace,
loose drainpipes beat themselves penitently
against the walls of taverns; and flies on their
        monuments
of dung rose and rattled like railings
in the blackened air. Even horsemeat
at the butcher's was properly spooked, and quivered
uncontrollably on slippery sirloin hooves.
So sudden the sound through our open window,
my grandmother's chicken soup clutched
at its noodles. But my stone-deaf grandfather sucked,
imperturbably gumless, at his pickled eggs.
In the entire town, only his apparently
unimportant adam's apple, bobbing
undeterred in a submarine motion, kept
the quiet and steady rhythm of the starry
universe, until the giant bells' swollen
metal tongues lolled exhausted
in their towers; and an evening rain fell
promptly, like a beneficent release of saliva,
as the last and greatest pickled egg
of all slid silently, and as duly
appointed, behind the surrounding bearded hills.

Old man in an armchair

After reading the day's newspaper, he would fold it
irrevocably, rasping each crease razor-sharp
with a rusty finger-nail; then, raising himself
      elaborately
on one leg and a multitude of elbows,
in a meticulously choreographed rheumatic ballet,
lodge it securely beneath the cushion of his seat.
No-one else could get at it. When a day
had looked through him thoroughly, its words were
      over
for everyone. Though his wife sometimes secretly
threw newspapers out at night,
his armchair went on rising imperturbably.
Sitting down became, for him, indistinguishable
from effortlessly standing up. Reclining
vertically, and almost motionless each day,
he was nevertheless undeniably going somewhere,
edging off from the corners of our sight.
He hovered eventually about as high as the
      mantelpiece,
with all the thoughtlessness life constantly
demands from us; keeping his balance perfectly
because he took it entirely for granted; falling
and breaking a hip only when walking
anxiously on the aggressively firm concrete
floor. Eventually, for his visiting grandchildren,
he spoke from the top of a mysterious tower
of rustling racing results and railway
disasters, just his white hair
shiningly visible to them in the after-school
gloom. For these grandchildren, he never quite
died, but simply levered himself off

through the attic window one night
between their visits, raising himself layer by yellowing
layer above the apple trees, until the cloud
that he humorously called his own hair
drifted majestically away with all
the white periwigs of the other prophets.

The street of gold

On Sabbath evenings, a slow hand
tuned the guitar. A fast hand
moved the shifting stars. And, somewhere,
while we were growing up, there was a street still
made of gold of tin of slush
of chrome of a bent geranium of hope
of a rusty euphonium (abandoned) of a torn
new dress, and, at the final corner,
Goldfaden's miraculous bakery, air
rippling like a tower of wheat above his roaring
chimney; and the chimney itself shaking as
                    argumentatively
as a suddenly cured cripple's unwanted
crutch, about to be hurled off forever
into the night. Whereupon the bakery would lurch
across the street, scattering a few
loose bricks, but mainly as many
cinnamon bagels as there are uncounted onions
or stars: bagels rolling all over
the place, faster than a three-speed bike,
and ending up, at a tilt, on everyone's
head, as jaunty and as fragrant as halos.

A MESSAGE FROM THE NORNS
TO THE TWENTY-FIRST CENTURY

Winter snapshot

A tram-car
stopped outside
in the big-petalled
snow, and bloomed
its bell, the air
thicker than daisies.

Puddle-hunting

At forty below,
a tire-print in snow
is a regimented cloud
of rubberized arrows, in flight
toward their distant quarry:
a trembling, but surely mythical,
mud-puddle.

Heavy rain

When it rains so hard, it is only the weather
remembering itself. Storms reminisce about other,
older, storms. Rains fall
within bygone rains. Gutters spout
on a grandfather's rested sight. That leak
in the scullery wall, it never got mended.
When we remember so hard, standing by the sinking
windows, it is only an unstoppable weather
that moves through our heads. Prints in the flower-
      bed
spill over with water, and recall one
drizzling fox back into place,
its nose whittled down to the fine point
of rabbit. Overhead, dripping pines
drift through each other in the mist, accumulating
times and places, countries and third
cousins' weddings, all as unavoidable
as the smell of wet mushrooms. When we remember
so hard, most of the rain that will fall
has long ago fallen, soaking ground
parched again, skies drained to a swampless
blue. Yet the remembered rain keeps on
pouring, on parents who are suddenly younger than
      us,
rain-coats glistening with surprise at their being wet
and alive once more. Their mouths move in their faces
like shining leaves, as they remind us repeatedly:
we must none of us ever stop raining.

Monsoon

I   A cloud beats on a small
      tight drum. The last
      apricots on the tree try
      to keep time. Gently,
      without falling off.

II   On a balcony overlooking the city,
      a girl, whose first love
      has again forgotten their assignation,
      brushes tidy tears
      discretely sideways, onto the pendants
      at her ears. They cluster there, shining
      in the evening's lungless heat.
      At last, a straining thread
      snaps. The first drops
      of monsoon rain scatter
      to the street below, like an overturned
      cart-load of berries.
      No-one jumps aside.
      Every sari is stained
      an uninhibited, thankful black.
      The girl uncovers and cools
      her knees. Calm comes back.

III   At sunset, a very rusty
      cloud above the rice-field
      ruptured like an unriveted tank.
      Only the water-buffalo
      stood his ground, head down,
      rain hosing hotly
      off his hide. By sunrise,
      after a night's steady cascade,
      he has turned triumphantly into a gleaming

grey boulder, cool
from the inside out, with just the slight
itchiness that boulders can have.

IV   During the long, dry summer,
lovers were moist with love
in the parched and yearning fields.
Now the rainy season has come,
they embrace harder, to keep dry,
huddled in the temple courtyard
under empty rice-sacks.

V   In the overflowing temple pond,
goldfish don't realize it is raining.
They know only that they have been
               wondrously
refashioned as birds. They fly
with poise through the previously unattainable
garden, flitting among frangipani.
A bedraggled temple-cat
hunches in a tree, sharpening
the five-fold mantra
of its claws, eyes hammering
to a hard green jade.

VI   In the temple courtyard, a beggar
plays on a bamboo flute.
He is its richest possession,
but the only one it needs.
He has the patience to perform all requisite
ceremonies for the streaming mud.
Rain on the roof-beam
chimes with anklets, dancing.
Wind strokes a sitar.

Phrases of the moon

Under the ascendancy of a full moon,
the woodcutter can find no trees,
only shadowless ways
of bearing stone leaves.

Whenever the moon passes behind a cloud,
lemons in the orchard all blink together,
and shoals of once-glittering herring
sink sootily under the sea.

Below a jagged new moon,
baths fill quietly
with slivers of broken glass
from empty wine bottles.

When the moon sets, inkwells
spill themselves over the countryside,
and steel nibs rust
deafeningly in empty libraries.

Yet whenever the moon rises, my girl
has eyes as green as olives,
arms as white as the reflection
of clouds in a saucer of cream.

When clouds canter by above the moon,
a stallion mounts his favourite
mare, and the scent of basil
and marjoram fills the air.

Under any kind of moon,
strings on a gypsy's guitar
turn into silver necklaces,
his voice into velvet gloves.

Five transformations of the moon

A desperate moon flung itself in the cistern.
A frog sticks its head through the moon.

The crescent moon rose
as our milk-cow, slowly
and massively, lifted her horns.

A pitcher of water on the table
—and an unrippled mirror of silence
covers the ceiling of the room.

Under a very full moon,
the heron devises flaring
matches from fish. They sizzle out.

On the city dump, the moon fills
empty jars with silver coins.
The jars wait for our lost gypsies
to return, and dance through the banks, investing
free fortunes in everyone's palm.

Trying to shout, in a market in Manchuria

In the market, the gaping carcass
of a calf swings on a hook.
Its life has become a huge
wide-opened mouth,
a red palate of ribs.
It tries to shout something.
—It can never stop trying.
But all that reaches us is rumour,
indistinguishable from a buzzing of flies;
the tongue already crammed down
by a very large cat.

The strong wind

Sometimes, a strong wind suddenly
swerves and drops beyond the headland.
Hulls leap to a surprised stop.
Sea sponges slowly suck out
blue from their anchors. While, on shore, flies
swarm knowingly onto everyone's shutters.

Sometimes, even anger stops suddenly
outside the oldest quarter of the town.
In half-open doorways, close-faced women
stare up at an alarming stillness
in the trees. Cats reappear, without
even moving, under the washing on the lines,
and contemplate a shining mantra in their claws.

Sometimes, hope comes to rest
just a street short of the match seller.
The smell of sulphur coils its corrosive
entrails around the unearned pennies in his head.
And in the back rooms of bordellos, fans
in the ceiling slap energetically at air
slowly going nowhere in the hot afternoon.

That strong wind of life, why
doesn't it reach us? The match seller
blows his nose in his palms, whistles
and hums. Somewhere, far out
at sea, a strong wind begins again,
terracing the waves into hanging gardens
of spray. Pray. Pray that we can stand
in that strong wind when, at last, it comes.

Heritage

We eat food from fields we did not clear.
Piled rocks look like unopened
letters, undelivered in the dry grass.
Then we moisten and exchange bodies on a strange
bed. The carved headboard twines us
together, in an unknown, varnished hand.
Afterwards, back on the street, the clouds
are, as usual, illegible, the drains unsigned.
We do not return to places we left.
A stranger sips coffee attentively there,
though the walls can't recall our names.
But we remember to be thankful, constantly, that
everything
important began with us. The shade
we sit in so romantically automatically throws
up the side of a shed, a broken rake
rotting beside it. We are our own heritage.
As leaves burn brown in the surprising
air of spring, may we be consistent
enough to forget to hand it on.

The presence of absences

Rameses II isn't buried
in the thundering silence of his tomb.
Even his glass case
at the Cairo Museum is empty.
He is away for repairs, to reattach
fingernails and visions to the brittle
kingdom. And we, too, do not live,
or even die, any more,
in our own lives. As we consume
this planet, bolting down
the shrinking remnant of everyone's
days, excavating around us
a sky-wide tomb,
our efficient actions reveal
the stern assumption that we live on,
and will inherit, another world,
safely elsewhere, though exactly
like this one; except that its days
will never be numbered. Our clothes
hang on us emptily. Our shoes
shuffle by themselves to the door.

A message from the Norns to the twenty-first century

Whatever certitude you have arrived at, we will over-
        rule.
The richness of the earth can be revoked. Mountains,
even, are being withdrawn. Mornings and evenings
may be done away with; their owls annulled
in mid-flight. Depths of oceans,
and the far greater depths of human song,
can be taken back, however warm
and dolphin-blue. Taken back, too, all
the ancient dead, unsaid completely
from their lives; and next year's children,
from their rescinded shawls. Skyscrapers and reactors
head our list, and will be recalled shortly,
falling through the upright air. Without the stroke
of a pen, we will quash whole continents
when we feel like it, and strike down nations
and their laws. Borders will be erased in forests
of pine that float off with the guards
in a dissolving mist. Not even their boots
will remain. The familiar sky is declared
redundant. Its constellations are being bent and
        rewoven;
the universe altered to another provisionally
hesitant form. Whatever certitude
you think you have reached, we have already over-
        ruled.

IN THE KOSHER CHOW MEIN RESTAURANT

Betting on history

The probability of any event's having happened
in the past shrinks with the passage of time.
It is already implausible that the pyramids were
            intricately
performed by Pharaohs, or any other
members of our lurching species, from such delicately
hewn huge snow-flakes of time,
unmelting in their hair's breadth geometry.
What chance that the Angles and Saxons ever arrived
in Britain, after what now seem wholly incredible
centuries of wandering westward through uncounted
lands; footprints on the riverbanks at dawn,
fires doused with their dreams? It is as likely
that they just began there in the hills, by a kind of
spontaneous uproar, pouring up
into sunlight from the grassy mounds that hatched
            them
at Sutton Hoo and elsewhere; growing
their treasures with them: cuttings for drinking horns,
golden seedlings for swords and brooches.
And do you really believe that the arrow hit
Harold smack in the eye at that fracas
near Hastings, when it was much more likely to have
            missed him
completely; or, perhaps, to have grazed him
            unromantically
in the thigh? The whole Norman Conquest
has the flavour of fiction. French words
in our language could more readily have come from
            the amorous
failures abroad of generation after generation
of English poets, who rhymed it so badly

with the girls of Grenoble, they just had to talk
both during and afterwards in bed: language
sprung from the sad lotteries of love.
It seems highly improbable that Drake was playing
bowls when the Armada was sighted. Bowls,
by the way, is already a chapter of accidents,
.and hardly appropriate to have properly existed.
Much more likely, he was groaning in the john;
or assiduously avoiding writing another
of those many very common late-arriving
letters, that help to make history a well-documented
speculation. Besides, mathematics maintains
it's impossible that so huge a fleet was ever
defeated. It still sails unstoppably on.
And the discovery of Canada by Vikings, or monks
meditating themselves in from China, is too incredible
to be accepted as a plausible coincidence. However,
our world leaders are doing their best
to make any future we may have as much of a turn
of the cards as the past, which is at least consistent.

Trying to balance the books

Too many roads made only for leaving on.
Too many jails built just for arriving.
Too many fires, but not enough
warmth in our fingers. Too much rain
on uncovered faces. Too much rain
on unburied faces. Too many battlefields
for all of the plowshares, plowing up
jaw-bones with languages smashed
in their teeth. Too many songs, with too few
singers. Too many interpreters of dreams,
without enough dreams to go round.
Too many politicians beating nothing
but words into plowshares, splintering their smiles.
Too many, or is it too few, saying:
everything's going to be all right.

1942

The SS officer raised his luger
gracefully, like a conductor's baton, when he came
to the ghetto's small orchestra. The first violin
fell forward into the suddenly quietened
ditch, still holding his twitching
bow and instrument. He didn't even start
at the pistol's crack, though his black coat
flew open with well-rehearsed ease
as he fell, and a raven rose from the woods
before his eyes sank in the mud. He left
nothing behind but its shadow, flapping
away across the cornfield, both seams
split from a vigorous love of playing.
Later, even the shadows were burned.

Borders

With the scratch of a pen, generals forthwith
divide mounting fox from eager
vixen in their den. The resulting cubs
can only catch mice that are officially tail-less.

At the border in the hills, customs-officers
try to turn back yet another
family of illegal clouds, each one
carrying a battered black suitcase of rain.

In cities that straddle two countries,
all the keyholes are turning into small wounds.
And inside the hotel-rooms, people grow
paler than ever, the carpets more luxuriantly red.

The migrating dust of the dead must carry
the dust of their passports in their crumbled hands.
Grave-markers will also be accepted,
but only if carved from the very best stone.

A secret machine will automatically guillotine
each gypsy song that changes
campfires and nations overnight. Fiddlers
are permitted to play only heavily sutured violins.

Will we still love the dances of their women,
red dresses swirling around a basketful of limbs?

Six reversals

I   Clothes hung to dry on the balcony
      have his body's shape. She day-dreams
           desperately
      that he will learn to make entangled love like
           that,
      sunning and dancing their unzippable bones,
      before some hidden line snaps.

II   Each morning, a girl and the sun walk by
      in the same orange dress. She leans
      against the old convent wall, waiting
      for a bus. When she leaves, the wall is held up
      entirely by its strapless memory of her back.

III   Arguments about religion can cause infidelity,
      sitting with someone you don't know,
      in a warm bath, listening to the pre-ordained
      street-car shuddering by outside,
      five secretive minutes late again.

IV   In the middle of the night, children's voices,
      layered beneath the hill that fell on their
           school,
      reach us faintly. They never stop playing.
      No-one had time to call them home.
      No words in their eulogies begged them to
           stop.

V   We return to make love again on the beach.
      But the sand has no memory of us beyond its
           last
      wave. And the next small ripple

hasn't heard if another will follow. Even life
gets so shallow here, a child couldn't swim in
      it.

VI   Spun around by storms, birds return
to nesting places they've never been in.
After many years, my father went back
to visit his birth-place. The town didn't know
he'd yet been born. He stayed and waited.

Where our voices go

Our voices go from us as we speak, fading
to the edge of the far field, yet still
as quietly insistent as the necklaces of November
sunlight on the wings of startled birds,
falling to whispers among the grass and nettles,
nudging questioningly among the nodding seedpods,
then lifting stray pollen, stammering it
that fraction further, trembling with the wind
in puddles whose shrinking memories can scarcely
hold on to their storms, seedpods
snapping at just that moment with the barely
perceptible pressure, seeds speaking
wider, voices travelling further out,
their speakers now successfully forgotten,
journeying in gathering crowds on clouds
of pollen, weaving intimately into
and out of each other, continuing every
speaker's conversation without his knowledge
or her permission, intonations making
allies, friends and complex marriages
that their original owners had never dreamt of,
giving birth to a faint lineage
of children in the eerie stir of hairs
on the backs of our over-proud and unsuspecting
        necks,
as we catch trains in opposite directions,
and succeed resourcefully in never truly
meeting, speeding further apart
as our words link syllables and cross
the muffled evening fields together,
the stars stuttering out, the harvest moon
huge but, as usual, strangely inaudible.

At the scene of the car-accident

By the roadside, a plastic bottle of cleaner
for contact-lenses is split and moulded
into a heel-less boot-print
in the mud; engineered by the accident to the exact
specifications of an eerily new thing:
the print of a being with long-striding
eyes for standing on—created only
for some alternate universe, and said,
by God, to be excellent there, not here.
A large garbage-bag in the ditch
looks like someone's son. Or laundry.
Clean? Or dead? Even God must stop
at the red police-flares, hoping not
to know the truth. Driving carefully,
on that day, and in this place,
was entirely a theological mistake, good
only on some other road, in another
year, in that parallel universe, where the branches
overhead are unable to move, even in the wind.
And the highway stretches backward, forever.

On a son's near escape from a car-crash

A day after his now flattened car
had effervesced off a sudden storm of washed-out
road, we drove our tightly-stitched
son back to the scene of the accident,
to look for his unloosed memories and belongings.
Where several sets of skid-marks
ended in the ditch, we found six
already well-weathered cassettes
of completely unfamiliar music, together
with his three tapes of rock-groups.
Short grass yielded his choices
easily; but thick thistles clung
officiously to the long-unheard bands.
This time, our son was lucky.
That particular stretch of Saskatchewan highway,
through waiting forests for fifty kilometres
on either side, extracted exact
tolls only from drivers playing
Albertan country-and-western medleys.
Such is the arbitrary bureaucracy of death.

Vagaries of memory at mid-winter

At mid-winter, in our parking lot,
a pink plastic comb lies
across a boot-print gripped by ice.
In the fading light, boot-print
and comb fumble to become a single
wholly new thing, uniting
to help bind the segments of this year
together as it crawls, cold and creaking,
toward the improbable puddles of spring.

It is then I remember, with the strained insignificance
of a second dropped comb, another
mid-winter, nearly fifty years ago.
At the end of a numbed war, at the far
end of a Cornish beach that was bandaged
with half-frozen spray, what I had thought
was yet another tar-blackened pig,
washed up beside a salt-chewed
sail, began to merge into the exact
shapelessness of a single well-drowned
sailor. The boy I was had begged then,
rather than prayed, that even a god would not step
closer to create and know the truth,
sweating suddenly from his gum-booted knees.

Now, at the close of this darkening year,
will reshaping shadows of the longest night
bring back familiar beaches
for the returning light, peopled with pigs
eagerly unbuttoning themselves from their swollen
dinner-jackets, and children to play around them?
Or sea-flayed sailors, too

tired to close their missing eyes?
Will I be bold enough to look and see,
on the unlit side of the morning newspaper,
propped against its convenient cereal packet?

Means and ends

When wars we are waging to protect
the peace are won, then all
five star generals
will be unmasked as saints and gardeners;
children chant from their embers
that they burned in an excellent cause;
and poisoned continents turn,
overnight, a delicate green again.

When we have shared our wealth fairly
by taxing the poor, banks
and newspapers will give away bread;
bemused dead have eyes
closed with newly minted
coins, and consider their hunger
well bought; slums be rebuilt
from rain and the very best mud.

Once we have freed the oppressed by murdering
their governments, girls' nightmares
will flood with carnivals of light;
landmines still in farmers'
fields issue guarantees
that they reattach arms and legs;
wells shine sweet again;
suns rise mostly for the just.

All we can say

All we can say, when love stumbles
to an end, is smoke rising from the hut
of the land-fill attendant on a windless day,
straight up like a question-mark into the sky.

When the judge pronounced a death-sentence,
the accused's only remaining plea
was the first hairs sprouting in his son's
armpits. But how could he say **that**?

When the phone rang to tell us a son
had rolled his car off the highway, our response
was the water that went on shaking at the sides
of its bowl, long after that had been set down.

Nowhere else but in my most lucid
dreams does the rabbi unmistakeably inform me
there are redheads in Ferraris only on the moon.
The billboards deliberately censor that fact.

The still-born child had its mouth
formed around the sound of fish holding
court in an unrippled pond at dawn.
It had accepted their ruling, without the need for
        appeal.

If you want to talk to a grandmother who's been dead
for years, the phone squats unresponsively
on the table. It hibernates like a misplaced frog,
until the feeling passes. Who's that, not speaking?

Outside death-row, in the grass
of summer, only the crickets speak.
Inside, the executioner takes up his trade,
and lets out an involuntary chirp.

What is man?

Man is made of what he can't shake loose
from his head. A mountain streaming with clouds
watches us whenever we speak. A river
creaks past on the hinges of its frogs.
The stars go on for ever with a silent
sound. The night claps one hand.

Man is whatever he desperately wants
to find: a girl, a gate, to be happier than he can.
He becomes that longing in a hungry height.
Then he feels through her eyes her turning from his
        hand.

He is what he often makes. A weaver
steps into the pattern of his rugs. Though he leaves
one loose thread each day,
to find the way back out.

Man can never know who he is.
He is always several hopes beside
himself. The bag-lady waiting
on the stairs is only looking for her life.

The final edict

There is an ancient edict issued by us that you have
    failed
to remember. This is the last reminder, and then we
    will act.
Our ruling was sealed clearly enough with shifting
sunlight, and edged by cliffs crumbling
continually into the high tides. Broken
gull chicks bear us good witness.
Our ordinance is that humankind shall migrate
    endlessly.
You are to be exiled by one inexhaustible hilltop
and valley after another. No forest is empowered by
    us
to let you stay. Why else were rivers
sent to administrate your wanderings? You are to be
    hunted
through mountains by the huge air's crackling
charge; and cast up by seas
in constipated estuaries of perpetually new
lands. Even your own bodies
you are to be banished from, through sleep and pain,
    and other
longer journeys. Hair thatched
on your heads can offer only occasional shelter.
You will blend with blurred oars you have pulled on
through generation after generation of splintered
    hands;
left to soften soapily on some lost
pebble strand. You will become stones
laid end to broken bone
in long-buried roads: your most enduring
points of departure. One day, perhaps,

you will climb to murder and perjury among the stars.
But all worlds have been instructed you are merely
a vagrant species. No planet,
however distant, can offer you permanent homes.
Do not dispute with us. Our decree is absolutely
fair and necessary. It applies to you all.
There are no appeals. We are the sole
tribunal. Our last signature will be the blue
thistle blooming in your factories; and stonecrop
spreading through your cities, putting them to rights.
It may take us time to rest our case against you,
but we can afford to be endless. Our edict, again, is
          this:
you shall wander as refugees from the cruelties in
          yourselves.
Unless you can change, and you never have yet,
our edict is final. Go, comply with it.

Preparations for a journey

Say goodbye to the people you never
managed to meet. And so long to the tombstones
in the oldest cemetery, held up unevenly
by hands already travelling in the dust.

Haul the keel closer to water.
The gravel clears its throat. Geese
fly overhead like schoolgirls trailing
their satchels. Late for school or love.

Lie at night listening to the hum
of the refrigerator. It perpetually leaves port,
shuddering ever closer to the tropic
of broccoli, light streaming on water.

Think of your grandfather marching off before you,
squeezing his mother's currant cake
into his knapsack. Crumbs rub shoulders
with loose ammunition. Which will explode first?

Enter narrow passages in strange
parts of the city. Step through shadows
as dark as bitter chocolate. In
and out of the rivers of memory and forgetfulness.

Discard in the centre of the room what cannot
be taken. That smell of burning leaves
that our fathers wore as their jackets. The cunning
of my right hand. The left side of my brain.

Give up your seat on an empty
tramcar. Kiss someone on lips
formed around a foreign language. Open
your windows. Break all the locks.

In the Kosher Chow Mein Restaurant

In this twenty-five course meal,
what is passed on from generation to generation
will never get lost: family assets
of the sun rising early over an old
and dented candlestick; of waters parting
strangely under junks on the Yangtze; of the
        candlestick
itself, floating in mid-air,
shedding several dented rays.

Things are placed carefully on the table.
A cup, a spoon, a prayer-book,
two chopsticks, a rabbi dancing
slowly on the tablecloth, and Lot's wife,
motionless, instead of a salt shaker.
Our waiter has the nose of Neferatiti,
the beard of Martin Buber, and eyes
that see through customers, like Ghengis Khan's.

In the kitchen, they translate ingredients from Ladino
to Yiddish to Cantonese to laughter, over a single
samovar of chicken noodle soup.
Streetlight streams through the slats of the blinds
like unnecessary interpretations of a Sigmund Freud,
illuminating hidden spiced mushrooms
in our dreams. Sometimes a cigar is just
a cigar; though my rice is a Ming tomb.

In secret proportions, cardamon from Yemen
is added to blessed rains falling
on the wheat fields of Manchuria; the rains,
in an unknown measure, to lovers across the table;

to passers-by in the street; to the trucks outside,
spitting curses through their air-brakes,
in yet another language that hurts
neither more nor less than "Adios, Susanna".

The ceiling is like a rice paddy of thick
grey plaster. Its surface heals
all our fractures, and hangs in their place
a wagon-wheel chandelier. Outside,
the traffic lights say "Sabbath",
"Go" and "Confucius", in quick succession.
The city is practising its mercy upon us.
It will not forget us, though we forget it.

Mung beans recite the Kaddish.
Peace upon my soul, and upon your red dress.
Amen, my skinny angel, who will not guard me
from all evil. Peace upon the moon-fish,
that was cooked in ginger. Peace upon my wrist,
that is strangled by my watch when your short dress
beholds me. Peace upon us from this place
to our place, from the restaurant to thy will be done.

My coat has fallen to the floor, I think,
my fallen name inscribed within it.
May strength shield us on dim corridors
to the cash-register. For tonight, kites
will soar above the shtetls, dragon-masks
peer cautiously round the corners of ghettos.
And, playing with grandparents, our children will
          demand
a very different fortune in their cookies.

CHRONOLOGICAL TABLE OF CONTENTS

ABOUT THE AUTHOR

Roger Nash was born in Maidenhead, England, in 1942.
Surviving the blitz, and being bombed out of his pram, he
was raised in Egypt and Singapore. He arrived in Canada in
1965, and has lived mainly in Sudbury since, though with
brief detours to Guelph, and to farm in the Tawatinaw
valley, Northern Alberta. He is a Canadian citizen.

Nash travels frequently, in the Middle East (Egypt, Jordan,
Israel) and Asia (Thailand, Hong-Kong, China—from
Guandong Province in the south, to Heilongjiang Province
in Inner Mongolia). These places, and the rich ethnic
diversity in Canada, help shape many of his poems.

He is married to psychologist and educator, Chris Nash.
They have two sons, Piers and Caedmon, both pursuing
careers in Bio-Chemistry.

Nash received a Ph.D. from the University of Exeter, and is
Associate Professor and Chair of Philosophy at Laurentian
University. He serves on the Board of the League of
Canadian Poets.

Roger Nash is available for poetry readings and talks
through:

> The League of Canadian Poets,
> 54 Wolseley Street, 3rd. Floor,
> Toronto, Ontario, M5T 1A5
> Phone: (416)504-1657; fax (416)947-0159

or at:

> Philosophy Department,
> Laurentian University,
> Sudbury, Ontario, P3E 2C6
> Phone: (705)675-1151